WORLD ADVENTURES

CONTENTS

BRICKS FOR ADVENTURE

In your world of adventure, anything is possible. Swinging vines, towering ships, and hi-tech robots all have a place in your LEGO® world. Here are some bricks that might be useful when building your fantastic adventures, but search your own collection for cool pieces, and use them! What else can you build?

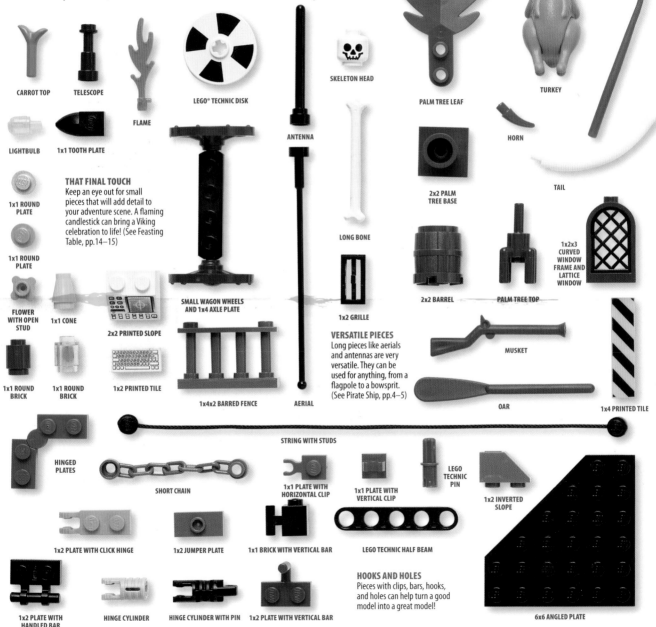

PLANT

VINE/WHIP

CARROT TOP

TELESCOPE

FLAME

LEGO® TECHNIC DISK

SKELETON HEAD

PALM TREE LEAF

TURKEY

HORN

LIGHTBULB

1x1 TOOTH PLATE

ANTENNA

2x2 PALM TREE BASE

TAIL

1x1 ROUND PLATE

THAT FINAL TOUCH
Keep an eye out for small pieces that will add detail to your adventure scene. A flaming candlestick can bring a Viking celebration to life! (See Feasting Table, pp.14–15)

LONG BONE

2x2 BARREL

PALM TREE TOP

1x2x3 CURVED WINDOW FRAME AND LATTICE WINDOW

1x1 ROUND PLATE

FLOWER WITH OPEN STUD

1x1 CONE

2x2 PRINTED SLOPE

SMALL WAGON WHEELS AND 1x4 AXLE PLATE

1x2 GRILLE

VERSATILE PIECES
Long pieces like aerials and antennas are very versatile. They can be used for anything, from a flagpole to a bowsprit. (See Pirate Ship, pp.4–5)

MUSKET

1x1 ROUND BRICK

1x1 ROUND BRICK

1x2 PRINTED TILE

1x4x2 BARRED FENCE

AERIAL

OAR

1x4 PRINTED TILE

HINGED PLATES

STRING WITH STUDS

SHORT CHAIN

1x1 PLATE WITH HORIZONTAL CLIP

1x1 PLATE WITH VERTICAL CLIP

LEGO TECHNIC PIN

1x2 INVERTED SLOPE

1x2 PLATE WITH CLICK HINGE

1x2 JUMPER PLATE

1x1 BRICK WITH VERTICAL BAR

LEGO TECHNIC HALF BEAM

HOOKS AND HOLES
Pieces with clips, bars, hooks, and holes can help turn a good model into a great model!

1x2 PLATE WITH HANDLED BAR

HINGE CYLINDER

HINGE CYLINDER WITH PIN

1x2 PLATE WITH VERTICAL BAR

6x6 ANGLED PLATE

RIGGING

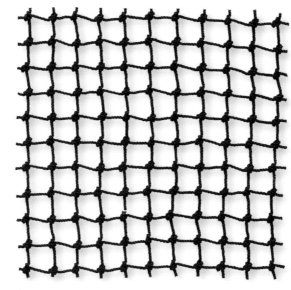

NET

LEGO TECHNIC RIM

LEGO TECHNIC
CROSS AXLE 8

SPIRAL TUBE

2x2 ROUND PLATE

2x2 RADAR DISH

BE ADVENTUROUS! BUILD WITH DIFFERENT TEXTURES, SHAPES, AND COLORS

2x2 ROUND BRICK

2x2 ROUND BRICK

1x2 RIDGED ROOF
CORNER SLOPE

CREATE WITH COLOR
Choose colors to help you
tell your story. Use gray
bricks for stone and rock,
brown for wooden
structures, green for
grass, and blue for
oceans and waterfalls!

4x4 ROUND BRICK

1x1x6 ROUND COLUMN

6x8x2 CURVED BRICK WITH HOLES

3x3 CURVED PLATE

STRANGE SHAPES
Unusually shaped bricks
and plates will make
your models interesting.
Try to use both big and
small pieces.

1x6 TILE   2x6 ANGLED SLOPE

2x12 PLATE

MAST

PIRATE SHIP

Ready to set sail for plunder and adventure, me hearties? Build yourself a mighty pirate ship! You'll need a tall mast with a sail and a fearsome skull and crossbones, a treasure hold for all your loot, a plank to make the landlubbers walk, a cannon or three, and, of course, a scurvy gang of buccaneers as crew!

BUILDING BRIEF
Objective: Make pirate ships
Use: Sailing the seven seas in search of treasure
Features: Masts, sails, pirate flags, cannons, planks, steering wheel
Extras: Figureheads, treasure chests, crew quarters, rigging

. . . .

A BOATLOAD OF BRICKS

There are all kinds of specialist pieces that you can use to build a pirate ship, from hulls to cannons to bowsprits, but here's a way to make one using mostly standard bricks and pieces.

Rudder is important for steering the ship

STEER CLEAR
The movable rudder is built from 1x2 bricks and 1x1 plates. Two clip plates attach it to bricks with vertical bars on the ship's squared-off back end.

Railings built from tiles and supported by 1x1 round bricks

REAR SIDE VIEW

Skull and crossbones pirate flag made from a skeleton minifigure head and bone accessories

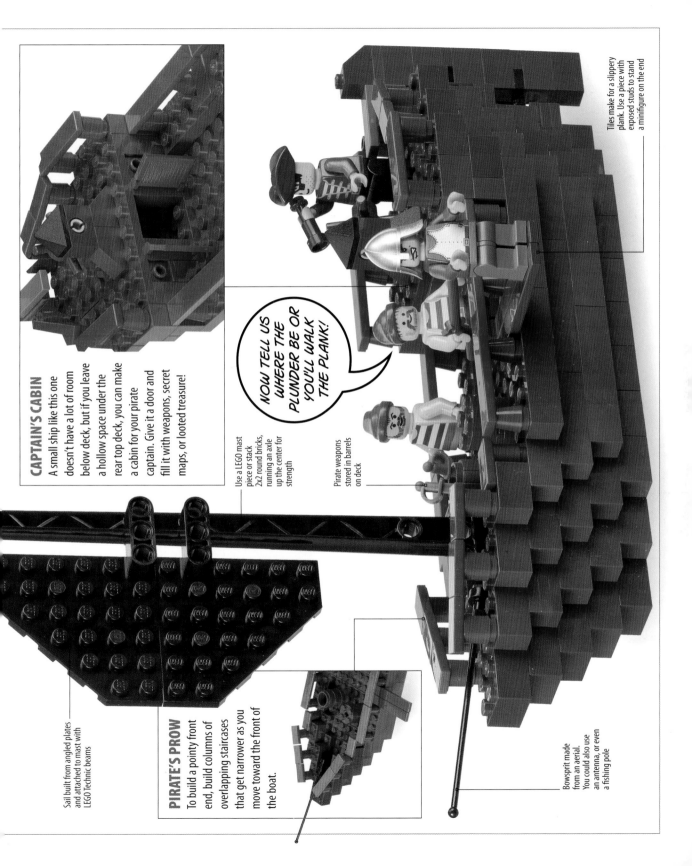

CAPTAIN'S CABIN

A small ship like this one doesn't have a lot of room below deck, but if you leave a hollow space under the rear top deck, you can make a cabin for your pirate captain. Give it a door and fill it with weapons, secret maps, or looted treasure!

NOW TELL US WHERE THE PLUNDER BE OR YOU'LL WALK THE PLANK!

Use a LEGO mast piece or stack 2x2 round bricks, running an axle up the center for strength

Pirate weapons stored in barrels on deck

Tiles make for a slippery plank. Use a piece with exposed studs to stand a minifigure on the end

Sail built from angled plates and attached to mast with LEGO Technic beams

PIRATE'S PROW

To build a pointy front end, build columns of overlapping staircases that get narrower as you move toward the front of the boat.

Bowsprit made from an aerial. You could also use an antenna, or even a fishing pole

A PIRATE'S WORLD

There is more to being a pirate than just sailing around in a ship! You can create an entire world for your bold buccaneers full of buried treasure, rival bands of pirates, cannon battles, and daring captures and rescues. There's plenty of swashbuckling action to be had!

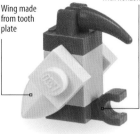

Wing made from tooth plate

Feet made from plate with horizontal clip

Beak made from horn

PARROTS

Every bad pirate should have a parrot! Start with a body of a 1x1 brick with side studs and clip on feet, wings, and a beak to create a colorful bird. You could use a 1x1 tile and feather pieces to add plumage.

BUILDING BRIEF
Objective: Add to your pirate world
Use: Expanding stories, adventures, and play ideas
Features: Places, vehicles, treasures, creatures
Extras: Pirate prison island, treasure cave

You could build a giant LEGO box to store your own valuables

Lock made from plate with handled bar

ALL THAT GLITTERS

Create treasure using transparent and metallic pieces for gems, coins, and gold. Make sure your treasure chest is big enough to hold it all!

> ARR, I'VE GOT THE TREASURE... NOW I JUST NEED A BIG HOLE TO BURY IT IN!

PIRATE TREASURE

You could make a removable lid, but why not use hinged bricks and plates to allow your chest to open and close? You could even add a keyhole by using a brick with a hole.

Plate with handled bar

Hinged brick and plate attaches lid to chest

TREASURE CHEST

Once you've found your treasure, you'll need somewhere to hide it away! You can build treasure chests in all shapes and sizes using plates and tiles that resemble wooden boards. Handles can be made using any piece a minifigure hand can clip onto.

PIRATE CANNON

Here's a cannon of a piratey variety. The flat platform and small wheel rims are ideal for rolling across the deck of a ship during a pitched sea battle.

READY... AIM... BUILD!

Rounded end-cap, made from domed brick

Cannon barrel built from 2x2 round bricks with LEGO Technic axle through the center

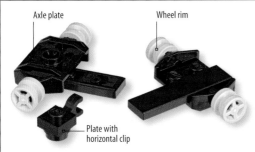

Axle plate

Wheel rim

Plate with horizontal clip

CANNON AID

For the cannon platform, attach wheel rims to upside-down axle plates held together by tiles. Then attach a clip to a handle on the cannon so it can tilt for aiming!

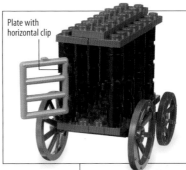

Plate with horizontal clip

LOCK-UP

A door hinge is created by building plates with horizontal clips into one of the bars of the cage. A single clip plate on the opposite bar makes a latch to close the door.

PRISON WAGON

Make a horse and wagon to whisk a captured pirate prisoner off to jail. For extra adventure, you could also build a secret hatch into the roof or floor for last-minute escapes!

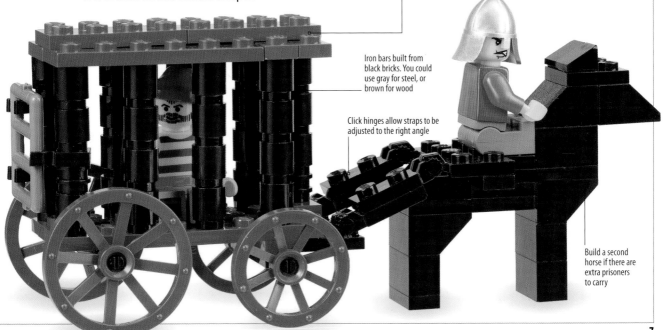

Iron bars built from black bricks. You could use gray for steel, or brown for wood

Click hinges allow straps to be adjusted to the right angle

Build a second horse if there are extra prisoners to carry

SHIPWRECK

Why not give your minifigures a pirate shipwreck scene to play in? You'll need a stormy sea, some ruinous rocks, and a pirate ship smashed to smithereens! Think of what else you could add to the scene—perhaps some floating treasure or escaping prisoners? You could even build a rowboat to rescue any survivors!

BUILDING BRIEF
Objective: Build shipwreck scenes
Use: A scene to pose or play with your pirate crew
Features: Wrecked ship, rocks, water
Extras: Seagulls, waves, floating debris

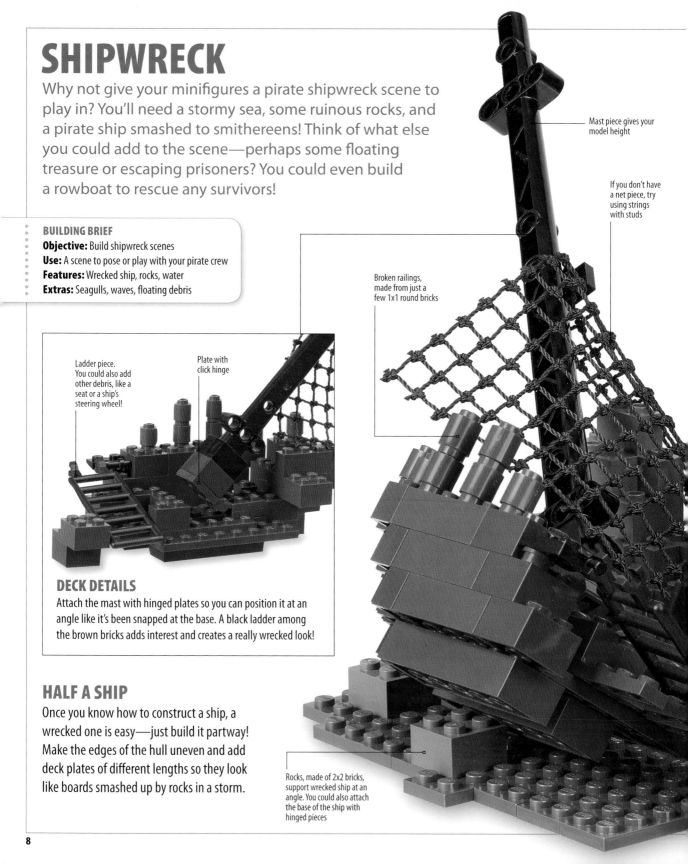

Mast piece gives your model height

If you don't have a net piece, try using strings with studs

Broken railings, made from just a few 1x1 round bricks

Ladder piece. You could also add other debris, like a seat or a ship's steering wheel!

Plate with click hinge

DECK DETAILS

Attach the mast with hinged plates so you can position it at an angle like it's been snapped at the base. A black ladder among the brown bricks adds interest and creates a really wrecked look!

HALF A SHIP

Once you know how to construct a ship, a wrecked one is easy—just build it partway! Make the edges of the hull uneven and add deck plates of different lengths so they look like boards smashed up by rocks in a storm.

Rocks, made of 2x2 bricks, support wrecked ship at an angle. You could also attach the base of the ship with hinged pieces

ROWBOAT

Build a rowboat just like you would make a pirate ship, but on a smaller scale. Use a rectangular brick or plate across two 1x2 bricks to make the pirate's seat.

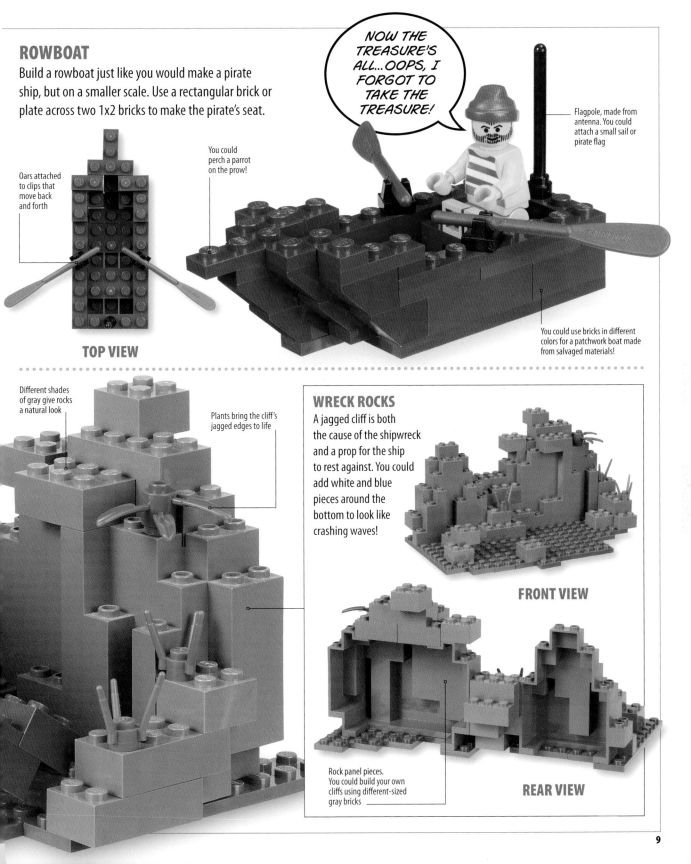

Oars attached to clips that move back and forth

You could perch a parrot on the prow!

NOW THE TREASURE'S ALL...OOPS, I FORGOT TO TAKE THE TREASURE!

Flagpole, made from antenna. You could attach a small sail or pirate flag

You could use bricks in different colors for a patchwork boat made from salvaged materials!

TOP VIEW

Different shades of gray give rocks a natural look

Plants bring the cliff's jagged edges to life

WRECK ROCKS

A jagged cliff is both the cause of the shipwreck and a prop for the ship to rest against. You could add white and blue pieces around the bottom to look like crashing waves!

FRONT VIEW

Rock panel pieces. You could build your own cliffs using different-sized gray bricks

REAR VIEW

9

PIRATE ISLAND

Even the most hardy sea dogs need somewhere to call home! Expand your pirate play with a pirate island. Imagine you're a pirate and think about what you might need in a hideout: How about a lookout for spotting enemy soldiers on the horizon? Or somewhere to moor your ship, or hide your treasure?

BUILDING BRIEF
Objective: Build a base for your pirates
Use: Storing booty, battling soldiers
Features: Island, weapons, dock, lookout
Extras: Jail cell, treasure, hidden weapons, pirate flags

PIRATE PATCH

You could build a fancy fort or a humble home for your pirates. This hideout has a simple but interesting design, with two main levels and a lookout level, all built on a small patch of land anchored in the middle of the sea.

A pirate fort needs weapons to protect it. This huge cannon should scare away any soldiers!

NEVER MIND SOLDIERS. HAS ANYBODY SEEN MY PARROT?

You don't need LEGO palm trees—make your own from brown 2x2 round bricks and leaf pieces

A base of blue sea gives way to yellow sand, then brown forest floor

Give your pirates a dock to moor their boats. Build it close to the fort for a quick getaway!

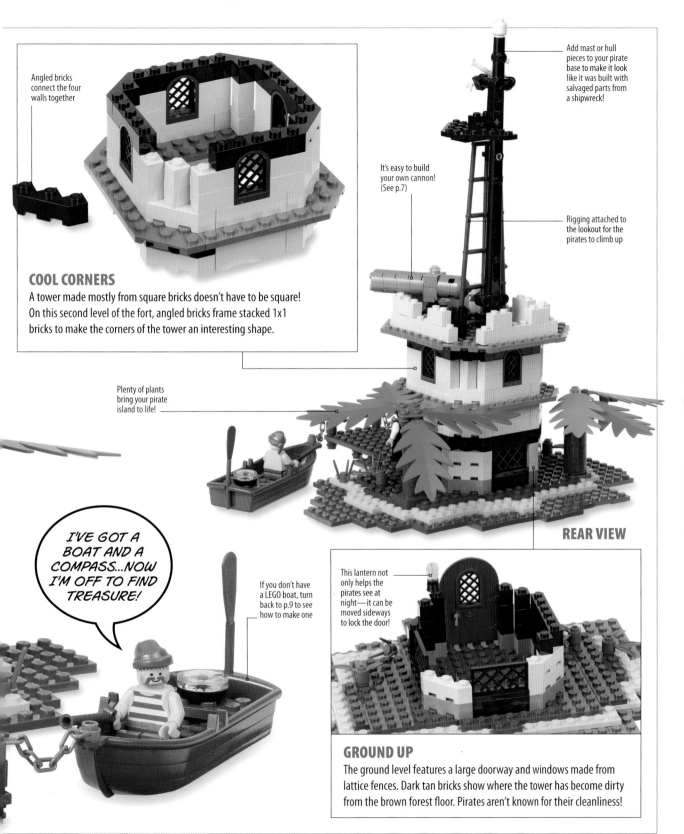

Angled bricks connect the four walls together

Add mast or hull pieces to your pirate base to make it look like it was built with salvaged parts from a shipwreck!

It's easy to build your own cannon! (See p.7)

Rigging attached to the lookout for the pirates to climb up

COOL CORNERS

A tower made mostly from square bricks doesn't have to be square! On this second level of the fort, angled bricks frame stacked 1x1 bricks to make the corners of the tower an interesting shape.

Plenty of plants bring your pirate island to life!

REAR VIEW

I'VE GOT A BOAT AND A COMPASS...NOW I'M OFF TO FIND TREASURE!

If you don't have a LEGO boat, turn back to p.9 to see how to make one

This lantern not only helps the pirates see at night—it can be moved sideways to lock the door!

GROUND UP

The ground level features a large doorway and windows made from lattice fences. Dark tan bricks show where the tower has become dirty from the brown forest floor. Pirates aren't known for their cleanliness!

VIKING LONGSHIP

Are your minifigures ready to set sail and conquer the world? They'll need a longship for their Viking adventures. Viking longships have a distinctive look, with low walls and a tall bow and stern, but the rest of the details are up to you. How many oarsmen do you need? What figurehead will you build at the front of your model? You could even add a second level to your ship, or billowing sails!

If you don't have a LEGO mast, you could build a stack of round 1x1 or 2x2 bricks

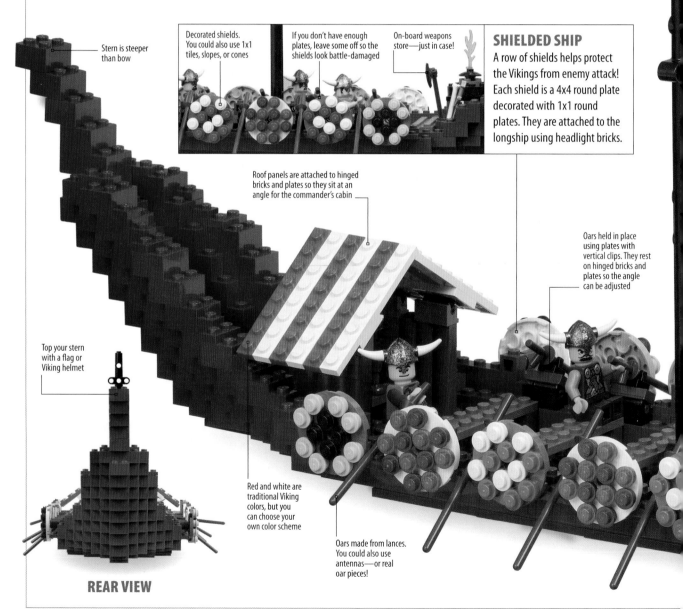

Stern is steeper than bow

Decorated shields. You could also use 1x1 tiles, slopes, or cones

If you don't have enough plates, leave some off so the shields look battle-damaged

On-board weapons store—just in case!

SHIELDED SHIP

A row of shields helps protect the Vikings from enemy attack! Each shield is a 4x4 round plate decorated with 1x1 round plates. They are attached to the longship using headlight bricks.

Roof panels are attached to hinged bricks and plates so they sit at an angle for the commander's cabin

Oars held in place using plates with vertical clips. They rest on hinged bricks and plates so the angle can be adjusted

Top your stern with a flag or Viking helmet

Red and white are traditional Viking colors, but you can choose your own color scheme

Oars made from lances. You could also use antennas—or real oar pieces!

REAR VIEW

MANPOWER

Viking ships are powered by a crew of strong oarsmen. Build a row of benches to seat the crew next to their oars. You could also add a furnace to provide light during the night.

This model is 16 studs wide. Decide how wide your longship will be. How many crew will it hold?

BOTTOM VIEW

Overlap plates to create a flat, sturdy base

A REALLY LONG SHIP

To get the shape of your longship right, start with a wide base of overlapping plates. Build the front and back sections separately using columns of stepped bricks that get narrower toward the bow and stern. Connect it all together at the base and secure with more plates if necessary.

Dragon head has white round plates for eyes and teeth

Flame held in place by a plate with vertical clip on top of a jumper plate

IF US DANES WANT TO CONQUER THE WORLD, WE SHOULD CONCENTRATE ON THE TOY MARKET.

Furnace built with log bricks, round bricks, and a radar dish on top

Curved neck built from stepped 2x3 bricks

This style of building is also used for the Pirate Ship (see pp.4–5)

Don't have enough brown bricks? Use different colors for Viking war paint!

VIKING VILLAGE

Even the toughest Viking needs somewhere to come home to after a long sea voyage. Build him a village and fill it with everything you think a Viking clan would need, including hearty food, fresh water, a welcoming fire, and a place to sleep. You could even build a wooden fence to protect the village from marauding enemies!

FEASTING TABLE

For a village feast, build long wooden tables and matching benches, then add as much food as you can find or build. Make it big enough for the whole clan to celebrate their Viking victories together!

THE FACT THAT WE FOUGHT THE BAD VIKINGS AND WON, REMEMBER?

SO WHAT ARE WE FEASTING ON THIS WEEK, GUYS?

Candlestick made from a telescope and a flame piece

If you don't have any Viking minifigures, combine armored bodies with bearded faces

14

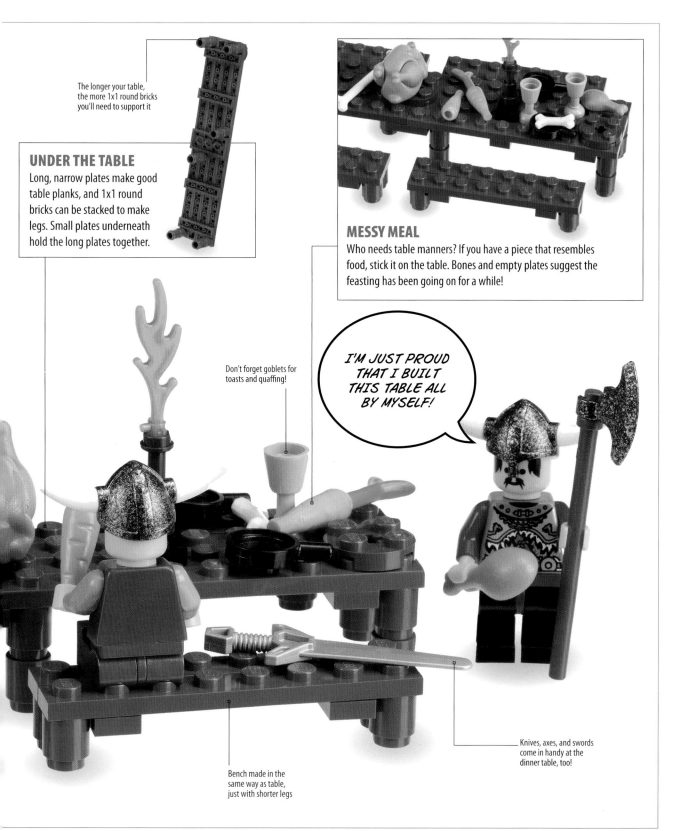

The longer your table, the more 1x1 round bricks you'll need to support it

UNDER THE TABLE
Long, narrow plates make good table planks, and 1x1 round bricks can be stacked to make legs. Small plates underneath hold the long plates together.

MESSY MEAL
Who needs table manners? If you have a piece that resembles food, stick it on the table. Bones and empty plates suggest the feasting has been going on for a while!

Don't forget goblets for toasts and quaffing!

I'M JUST PROUD THAT I BUILT THIS TABLE ALL BY MYSELF!

Knives, axes, and swords come in handy at the dinner table, too!

Bench made in the same way as table, just with shorter legs

JUNGLE ROPE BRIDGE

You may never have been to a jungle, but everyone knows what they look like. Lots of green leaves, plants, and vines. Ancient, twisted trees. Rivers and waterfalls. There are so many possibilities! And when you create the natural world in bricks, you can be as freeform as you like—if you haven't got enough pieces to finish a tree, leave it as a stump!

Vegetation, placed on irregular tree surfaces for a natural effect

String passes through the middle slat so the rope bridge keeps its shape. It hangs loose elsewhere

This is a great piece to make a jungle vine, which only needs one stud. You could also build clips into your tree to attach extra plants

ROPE BRIDGE

The coolest way to cross a jungle river is by rope bridge! This one is made from four lengths of string with studs on the ends. The slats are brown 1x4 plates. The trees are made from bricks, inverted slopes, and plant leaves, arranged to look random and natural, with lumps and bumps all over.

Bumpy forest floor, created using brown and green plates arranged in an irregular pattern

Access to the bridge is via a ladder, attached to the tree with a plate with handled bar

FALLEN LOGS

Logs fall on the forest floor and plants grow around them. Side branches may also have leaves growing from them. These leaves grow in different directions, which is what this model is replicating.

Logs can be strewn around your jungle scene for extra realism

CLIP-ON LEAVES

The central trunk of the log is made from brown 2x2 round bricks. Then, a 1x1 plate with horizontal clip is fitted in so the plants can grow upward from the trunk.

1x1 round bricks form side branch

2x2 round brick

1x1 plate with horizontal clip

CAMP FIRE

Here's a camp fire for cooking or warmth—even the jungle can get cold at night. Brown 1x1 round bricks form the logs and robot arms and tube studs hold the flames.

If you don't have flames, you could create smoldering embers with any small red and orange pieces

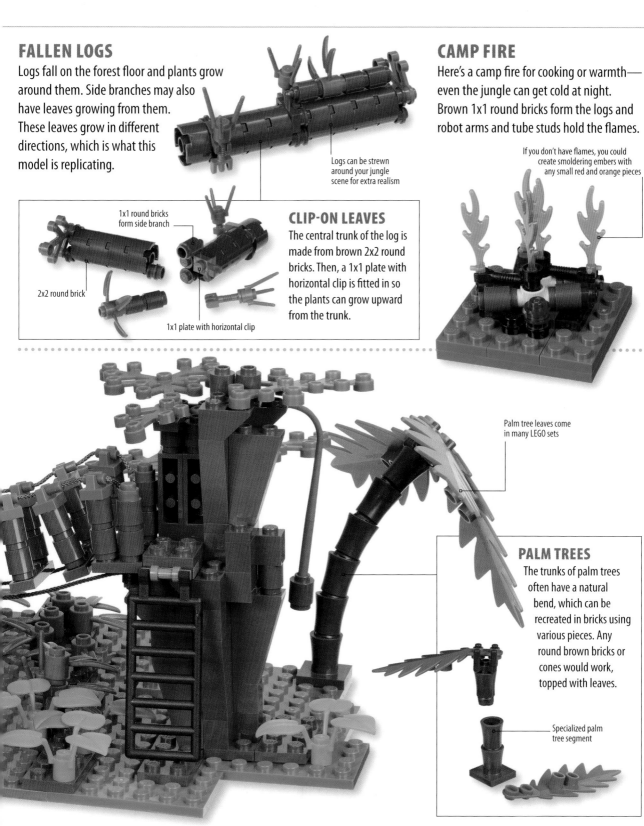

Palm tree leaves come in many LEGO sets

PALM TREES

The trunks of palm trees often have a natural bend, which can be recreated in bricks using various pieces. Any round brown bricks or cones would work, topped with leaves.

Specialized palm tree segment

INTO THE JUNGLE

Time to expand your jungle landscape! You can add mystery and adventure by building ancient ruins, and long-lost forbidden temples. Not everything has to be man-made, either—how about a raging river full of snapping crocodiles or a rushing waterfall? Go wild with your creations!

BUILDING BRIEF
Objective: Expand your jungle
Use: New places to play and explore
Features: Crumbling ruins, waterfalls
Extras: Jungle animals, trees, mountains

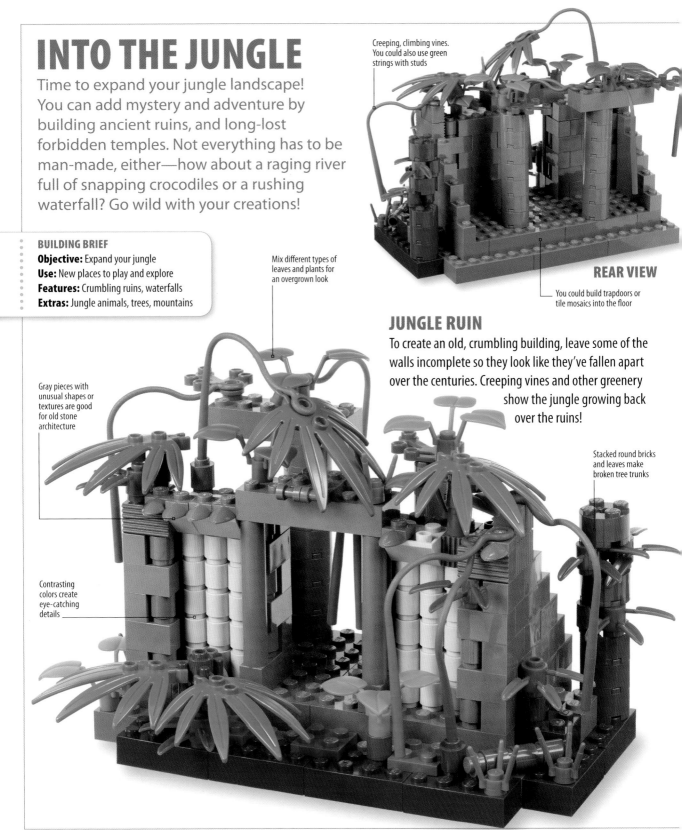

Creeping, climbing vines. You could also use green strings with studs

REAR VIEW

You could build trapdoors or tile mosaics into the floor

Mix different types of leaves and plants for an overgrown look

JUNGLE RUIN

To create an old, crumbling building, leave some of the walls incomplete so they look like they've fallen apart over the centuries. Creeping vines and other greenery show the jungle growing back over the ruins!

Gray pieces with unusual shapes or textures are good for old stone architecture

Stacked round bricks and leaves make broken tree trunks

Contrasting colors create eye-catching details

Jagged rock face
built as a cluster
of gray bricks

Use narrow plates for a
gentle trickle or layers of
narrow and wide plates
for a rushing torrent

JUNGLE WATERFALL

To create a waterfall, first build a rocky base,
then add blue bricks for running water.
The coolest part is making it look like it's
really flowing downhill.

FALLING WATER

The stream of this waterfall is made with
one-stud-wide blue plates built onto plates
with click hinges. Hinges allow the waterfall
to be angled so it flows down the rocks. If you
don't have hinges, try building the blue
pieces directly onto the rock face.

You could expand the
pool at the bottom and
create a jungle lake scene

Plants grow at the
well-watered base. You could
add flowers or trees, too!

GRAND ENTRANCE

The temple gate is built from a
barred fence turned sideways.
It is clipped to an antenna that
is secured in the doorway.
Use a plate with handled bar
for the door handle.

Plate with handled bar

You can build the
temple as large
as you want!

You could completely
cover your temple
with vegetation and
vines so it looks lost
and forgotten

LOST TEMPLE

Even a small jungle building can
make a big impact. This secret temple
may look like an ordinary pile of
rocks, but the barred gate hints that
something important is hidden
inside. What that is...is up to you!

Add secret treasure, a long-lost explorer,
or a hidden tunnel inside the temple.
What else can you think of?

WILD ANIMALS

Fill your jungles, plains, and savannas with wild animals of all species! Identify the shapes, proportions, and patterns of your chosen animal and try to stick as close to the real thing as you can! The more you can show what makes the animal unique, the better your model will be!

BUILDING BRIEF

Objective: Make animal models
Use: Living in a jungle, zoo, or desert
Features: Stability, distinct features
Extras: Opening jaws, moving limbs

Eyes, ears, and horns attach to bricks with side studs

GIRAFFE

A giraffe's most recognizable feature is its long neck. Use a variety of bricks and slopes to get the body shape and markings just right. You could build a bigger head so you have more room for facial features.

You could build a longer neck, but remember, the longer it is, the less stable it will be!

Real giraffe spots aren't regular, so make your model's pattern look random

Inverted slope creates natural shapes at base of neck and top of legs

Pointy hooves, made from tooth plates. You could use round plates for small hooves

Tail, legs, and neck are stacks of 1x1 bricks and plates

Studs on back resemble tough elephant skin

If you don't have these tail pieces for tusks, try a curved half arch

ELEPHANT

Big ears, big tusks, big trunk, big legs—everybody knows what an elephant looks like! With so many parts sticking out, make sure they're all attached securely.

If the trunk is too heavy to stay attached, build it all the way down to the ground

2x3 curved plate with hole

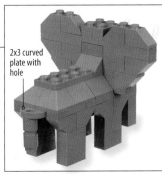

STAYING STURDY

The ears are built into the sides of the head for stability. The tail is two round bricks hanging from a 2x3 curved plate with hole, which is built securely into the body.

CROCODILE

This hungry reptile looks like it's floating in water, with only the top half of its body visible. To build a crocodile on land, add a belly, lower jaw, and the rest of the tail and legs!

Half-submerged teeth made from round plates

Spikes built from green ridged roof corner slopes

Tail and legs built with hinged plates for posability

Zebra's nose built from ridged roof corner slopes

Body built from 1x2 slopes held together by plates underneath

1x2 slopes help to give the legs shape

AS I SAID TO MY LEOPARD FRIEND, STRIPES ARE THE NEW SPOTS!

ZEBRA

Here's a solid little zebra you can build entirely out of black and white pieces. Alternate the colors to create a stripy model!

Striped legs made from stacks of alternating black and white plates

ROBOTS

When building robots, anything goes! They can be simple or complicated, silly or cool. Who needs normal feet when you can roll around on wheels or clank across the floor with big stompers? Use hinges, joints, and turntables to add posability, and try adding printed tiles, radar dishes, and LEGO Technic pieces for mechanical details!

YOU CAN'T MISS ME, EVEN IN A CROWD OF ROBOTS!

BUILDING BRIEF
Objective: Build robots of all shapes and sizes
Use: Heavy lifting, major computation, battle
Features: Movable sections, tools
Extras: Swappable parts, lights, motorized functions

You don't have to leave all the rims bare—add some tires for a rounder, bouncier robot!

Angled LEGO Technic pieces make good robot shoulders

Outer rims rotate around axle to swing legs

Short LEGO Technic axles for fingers

WHEEL-BOT

This curious little robot is built out of wheel rims held together by LEGO Technic axles and pins. Its head and limbs can rotate, and the entire thing can fold up into a power-down mode. If you want to make a really big robot, use lots of bricks to make each part of your robot's body. Don't forget to make sure you have at least two of each piece for the arms and legs so that both sides match!

LEGO Technic rims built up together make chunky legs

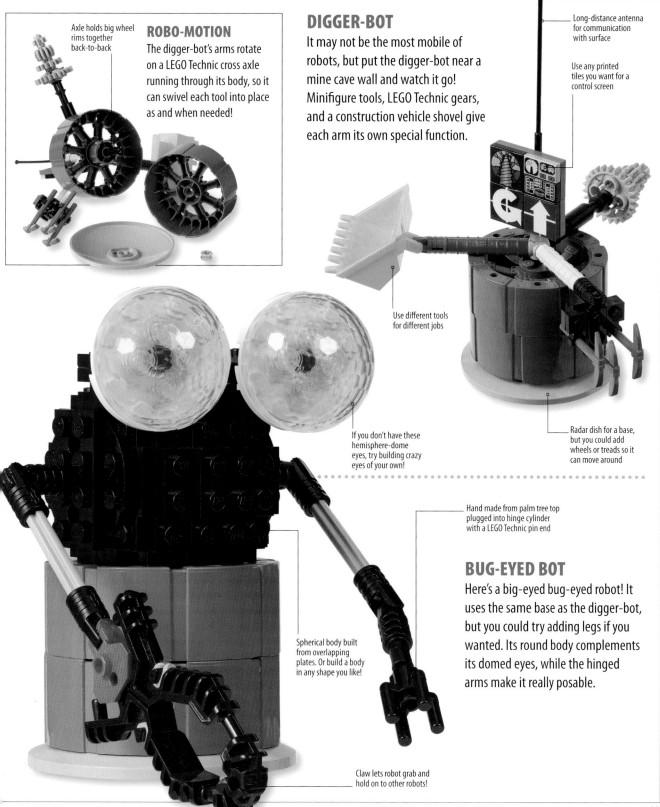

ROBO-MOTION

Axle holds big wheel rims together back-to-back

The digger-bot's arms rotate on a LEGO Technic cross axle running through its body, so it can swivel each tool into place as and when needed!

DIGGER-BOT

It may not be the most mobile of robots, but put the digger-bot near a mine cave wall and watch it go! Minifigure tools, LEGO Technic gears, and a construction vehicle shovel give each arm its own special function.

Long-distance antenna for communication with surface

Use any printed tiles you want for a control screen

Use different tools for different jobs

Radar dish for a base, but you could add wheels or treads so it can move around

If you don't have these hemisphere-dome eyes, try building crazy eyes of your own!

Hand made from palm tree top plugged into hinge cylinder with a LEGO Technic pin end

BUG-EYED BOT

Here's a big-eyed bug-eyed robot! It uses the same base as the digger-bot, but you could try adding legs if you wanted. Its round body complements its domed eyes, while the hinged arms make it really posable.

Spherical body built from overlapping plates. Or build a body in any shape you like!

Claw lets robot grab and hold on to other robots!

CREATURE 'BOTS

Robots don't need to have arms, legs, or even heads. They can be wide, skinny, tall, short, huge, or tiny. They can resemble real-life creatures or look like nothing you've ever seen before! Use unusual pieces to create your creature 'bots—the crazier the better!

BUILDING BRIEF
Objective: Build the wildest robots you can imagine
Use: Experimentation, fun
Features: Unusual bricks used in new ways
Extras: Mad science lab, robot testing chamber

You could add functional accessories to the tip of the tail, like a computer screen or spy camera!

Plug in an antenna for a long tail

Use clips to attach weapons or equipment to bars all over body

Posable legs can fold under the body while in flight

Want to go faster? Substitute rocket boosters for wings!

LIZARD-BOT

Robots don't necessarily need solid bodies. This flying lizard robot is built from ladders, grilles, and other skeletal frame pieces, all held together by clips and bars. Printed tiles provide cool computerized controls!

BOTTOM VIEW

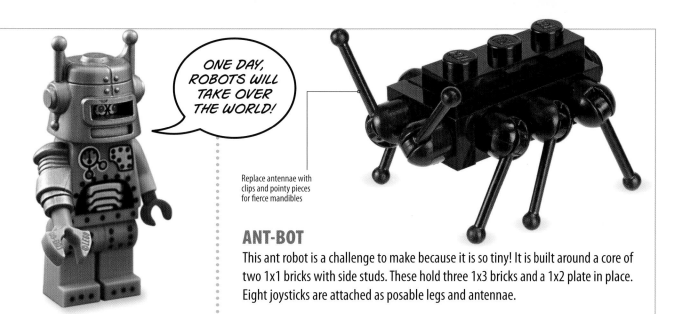

ONE DAY, ROBOTS WILL TAKE OVER THE WORLD!

Replace antennae with clips and pointy pieces for fierce mandibles

ANT-BOT

This ant robot is a challenge to make because it is so tiny! It is built around a core of two 1x1 bricks with side studs. These hold three 1x3 bricks and a 1x2 plate in place. Eight joysticks are attached as posable legs and antennae.

You could add a seat so a minifigure can fly on the lizard-bot

Head made from cockpit rollcage

REAL-WORLD ROBOTS

Robots aren't only from science fiction. They're all around us in the world today—assembling cars, working with dangerous objects, exploring the depths of the ocean and outer space, and performing all kinds of other tasks that human beings can't safely do. When building a real-world robot, think about its function and what kind of design and tools it needs to do its work!

Welder made from spear

Stack round bricks with a LEGO Technic axle through the center as a support column

Try adding 2x4 or 2x2 bricks under the yellow stack for extra stability

Use printed tiles to make computer consoles and readouts

CAR FACTORY ROBOTS

Industrial robots don't have to look pretty; they just have to get the job done. This auto assembly system is built in three parts: the robot workers, the car frame, and the conveyor belt.

AUTO INCOMPLETE

The in-progress car is made out of plates with click hinges and tiles arranged in the outline of a car. You can leave even more parts out, since it's still being built.

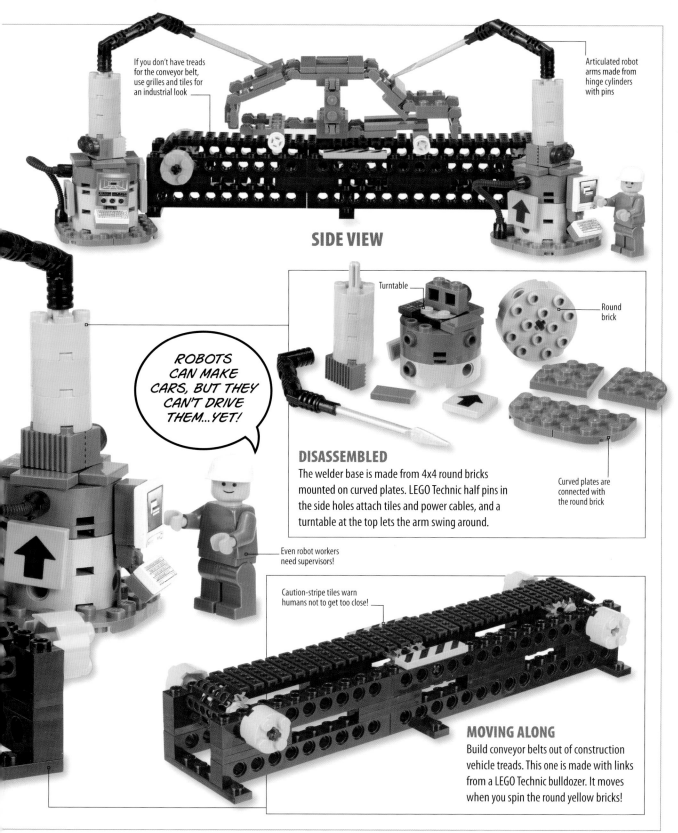

If you don't have treads for the conveyor belt, use grilles and tiles for an industrial look

Articulated robot arms made from hinge cylinders with pins

SIDE VIEW

Turntable

Round brick

ROBOTS CAN MAKE CARS, BUT THEY CAN'T DRIVE THEM...YET!

DISASSEMBLED

The welder base is made from 4x4 round bricks mounted on curved plates. LEGO Technic half pins in the side holes attach tiles and power cables, and a turntable at the top lets the arm swing around.

Curved plates are connected with the round brick

Even robot workers need supervisors!

Caution-stripe tiles warn humans not to get too close!

MOVING ALONG

Build conveyor belts out of construction vehicle treads. This one is made with links from a LEGO Technic bulldozer. It moves when you spin the round yellow bricks!

DK | Penguin Random House

Editor Shari Last
Additional Editors Jo Casey, Hannah Dolan, Emma Grange,
Matt Jones, Catherine Saunders, Lisa Stock, Victoria Taylor
Senior Editor Laura Gilbert
Designer Owen Bennett
Additional Designers Lynne Moulding, Robert Perry,
Lisa Sodeau, Ron Stobbart, Rhys Thomas, Toby Truphet
Jacket Designer David McDonald
Senior Designer Nathan Martin
Senior DTP Designer Kavita Varma
Producer Lloyd Robertson
Managing Editor Simon Hugo
Design Manager Guy Harvey
Creative Manager Sarah Harland
Art Director Lisa Lanzarini
Publisher Julie Ferris
Publishing Director Simon Beecroft

Photography by Gary Ombler,
Brian Poulsen, and Tim Trøjborg

Acknowledgments
Dorling Kindersley would like to thank: Stephanie Lawrence, Randi Sørensen, and
Corinna van Delden at the LEGO Group; Sebastiaan Arts, Tim Goddard, Deborah
Higdon, Barney Main, Duncan Titmarsh (www.bright-bricks.com), and Andrew
Walker for their amazing models; Jeff van Winden for additional building; Daniel
Lipkowitz for his fantastic text; Gary Ombler, Brian Poulsen, and Tim Trøjborg for
their brilliant photography; Rachel Peng and Bo Wei at IM Studios;
and Sarah Harland for editorial assistance.

First published in the United States in 2015 by DK Publishing
345 Hudson Street, New York, New York 10014

Contains material previously published in
The LEGO® Ideas Book (2011)

001—284611—Mar/15

Page design copyright © 2015 Dorling Kindersley Limited.
A Penguin Random House Company.

A catalog record for this book is available from the Library of Congress.

ISBN: 978-5-0010-1311-2

Printed in China.

www.dk.com
www.LEGO.com

A WORLD OF IDEAS:
SEE ALL THERE IS TO KNOW